THE STORY OF WEREWOLVES

OTHER BOOKS BY THE AUTHOR

THE STORY OF Werewolves

THOMAS G. AYLESWORTH

illustrated with photographs and old prints

McGRAW-HILL BOOK COMPANY

New York • St. Louis • San Francisco • Montreal • Panama • Toronto

To Barthold Fles: Wise counselor,
Lover of books, Good friend.

Library of Congress Cataloging in Publication Data

Aylesworth, Thomas G.
    The story of werewolves.

    Bibliography: p.
    Includes index.
    SUMMARY: Includes a brief description of the physical characteristics
and history of werewolves and a collection of werewolf legends from all
over the world.
    1. Werewolves—Juvenile   literature.   2. Tales.   [1. Werewolves—
Fiction.   2. Folklore]   I. Title.
PZ8.1.A89St   [398.2]   78-8226
ISBN 0-07-002645-9

TABLE OF CONTENTS

1

WHERE DID IT COME FROM?

Hardly anybody believes in werewolves today. But there was a time when many people did. Especially the people who lived in Europe, parts of Asia, and certain places in North America.

Usually, a werewolf is a man or woman who turns into a wolf. And this is supposed to happen only on certain days of the month when there is a full moon. When the change happens, he or she becomes a man-killing beast. But the werewolf keeps a human ability to reason. And sometimes it can even talk. When the sun comes up, the werewolf turns back into a human.

Werewolves are monsters. That means that they are different from vampires, ghosts, demons, and devils. Werewolves and other monsters are alive. Vampires and other ghosts are dead. Demons and devils never were alive.

But where did all those strange stories about werewolves come from? They might go as far back as the days of the cave people. It seems that man has always been deathly afraid of wolves; and with good reason.

Wolves often travel in packs. And they often roam about at night. (That's the time when it is easiest to be afraid of something.) They move in ghostly silence, except when they start their frightful howling. They have slanting eyes that may glow yellowish-green in the moonlight or red in the firelight. And they eat living things.

In the Bible, you can find references to the wolf. Matthew says, "Beware of false prophets, who come to you in clothing of sheep, but inwardly they are ravening wolves."

Wolves were thought to be cruel and fierce.

Werewolves were usually thought to be fierce. Here is a picture of one going about his business. It comes from *The Book of Were-wolves*, written by Sabine Baring-Gould, published in 1864. The author was a minister who was most famous for writing the hymn, *Onward Christian Soldiers*.

Remember how they acted in *Little Red Riding Hood* and *The Three Little Pigs*?

Centuries ago, in Greece, there were stories about werewolves. Homer and Plato, two ancient Greek writers, told of the nasty character of the wolf. And the Greeks believed that when they died, their souls crossed the River Styx on a ferryboat. The ferryman of that boat was named Charon, and he was said to wear a wolfskin robe.

The Romans improved the legend of the

The ancient Greek werewolf, Lycaeon, from a sixteenth-century engraving.

werewolf. Ovid, a Roman poet, wrote about Lycaeon, the King of Arcadia. The story goes that Lycaeon invited Jupiter, the chief god of the Romans, to a party. He surprised Jupiter by serving him a stew of human flesh. The god was so angry that he turned Lycaeon into a werewolf. To this day, the act of turning into a wolf is called *lycanthropy* (lye-CAN-thro-pee), in honor of that unfortunate man.

Werewolf stories from Great Britain go back a long way, too. There is a legend that St. Patrick, the patron saint of Ireland, was involved in lycanthropy in the fifth century A.D. Some people believed that he changed Vereticus, the King of Wales, into a werewolf.

There is a reason why the ancient Britons believed in werewolves. At that time, huge forests could be found all over the British Isles. Some of them stretched for eighty miles or more. These forests contained some of the swiftest and most savage wolf packs that you can imagine.

One of the favorite sports of the ancient Britons was wolf-hunting. The Saxons, another ancient tribe, called the month of January *Wolf-monat*, or "wolf month." January was the month when the wolves were the hungriest because so many of the animals they ate were hibernating. And so they were at their fiercest.

So the belief in werewolves grew. In 766, a law was passed by the Church. No one could eat the meat of cattle that had been killed by wolves because it might be contaminated. In the 900's, King Athelstan went even further. He built what was called a "Hospital for the defense of way-faring people passing that way from Wolves, lest they should be devoured."

In the 1100's, the Bishop of Exeter told people to study lycanthropy. In the 1200's, John of Lackland, an evil king, was said to be a were-wolf. The story goes that, after his death, strange sounds came from his tomb. His body was uncovered and thrown on the ground. At that moment he turned into a wolf.

One of the strangest werewolf stories of that time is an Irish tale. A priest and a young man were traveling through a forest. One night, just before they were going to sleep, a wolf appeared. The wolf told them that there was nothing to fear, but he confessed that he was really a werewolf. And so was his wife.

They had been cursed, and changed into wolves every seven years. Now his wife was dying in another part of the forest. The wolf asked the priest to go and give her the last rites of the Church.

The priest went to the dying wolf and comforted her. But he could not bring himself to give her the communion wafer.

Then the wolf-husband tore off part of his wife's skin. The priest could see that under the fur was the body of an old woman. He gave her the wafer and her husband was able to remove the rest of the wolf's skin.

More and more stories were told in the British Isles. And the war went on between men and wolves. Wolf hunts were held and money was paid for wolves' bodies and skins. The Irish wolfhound was bred in Ireland just to kill wolves. By the 1700's, there were almost no wolves left there.

The British were not alone. The Latvians and the Estonians believed that whole packs of werewolves would wander around the countryside. Just after Christmas Day, two strangers would appear—a lame boy and a tall man. The boy traveled about, telling all the evil people to follow him. Anyone who refused would be punished. The tall man would beat them with a whip made of iron chains.

When they started to follow the boy, the people would change into wolves. It was said that these groups might number in the thousands.

As the wolves marched along, they killed all the cattle that they found. But they did not eat humans.

Sometimes they would come to a river. Then

Another ancient version of a werewolf. Here the beast is seen attacking a favorite victim—the young girl.

the tall man would hit the water with his whip. The water would part, allowing the werewolves to walk across the river on dry land. The procession was said to last for twelve days, after which everyone turned back into human form.

The Germans also had their beliefs. During the 1500's, many German priests asked an embarrassing question during confessions. They would enquire, "Do you believe that people can become werewolves?" At that same time, a series of lectures was given in Germany. The purpose of the talks was to explain lycanthropy to the people. And the belief in these beasts, in some parts of Germany, was still strong until the middle of the 1800's.

So now you know some of the background. And it's all related to man's fear of the wolf. The wolf was seldom a nice fellow in folklore. He slobbered. He was cruel. He had a huge appetite. He was strong, he was smart, and he was fast. Who wouldn't be afraid of him?

Fear of the wolf made people hysterical. They wanted to destroy it. The wolf was hunted so widely that it has almost vanished from Britain, Germany, Switzerland, France, and the United States.

Today, many people are still afraid of these animals. Who can blame them? As recently as one hundred years ago in Russia, one hundred sixty people were killed by wolves in one year alone.

Some peasants in Sweden are in the same boat. They are so frightened of the beast that they will not speak the word for "wolf." They call the animal "The Gray One."

So here was the situation not so long ago. More people were afraid of wolves then than they are today. They also believed in demons, witches, vampires, and lots of other spooky things. People also thought that humans could be changed into other types of animals. Under these conditions, what could be more believable than the legend of the werewolf?

Over the years, werewolf stories were told in many different countries. The word *werewolf* seems to come from two Anglo-Saxon words, *wer* and *wolf*. In that language, *wer* means man. In other countries, this man-wolf had different names.

In Germany, it was the wer-wolf (VARE-VOOLF)
In Spain, it was the lob hombre (LOHB OHM-bray)
In Portugal, it was the lobh omen (LOHB OH-mayn)
In Brittany (a part of France), it was the bisclaveret (bees-CLAH-vayr-ay)
In Italy, it was the lupo manero (LOO-poh mah-NAY-roh)

11

In Greece, it was the vrykolaka (vree-KOH-lah-kah)
In Scandinavia, it was the varûlf (VAHR-oolf)
In France, it was the loup-garou (LOO gahr-oo)
In Bulgaria, it was the vrkolak (VER-koh-lahk)
In Slovakia, it was the vlkodlak (VUHL-koh-dlahk)
In White Russia, it was the wawkalak (VAHV-kah-lahk)
In Central Russia, it was the bodark (BOH-dark)
Among the Mohawk Indians it was the limikkin (LIM-i-kin).

The werewolf legend never did seem to lend itself to novelists. There really aren't a large number of fictional books about the wolfman. But the movies have had a field day with the creature.

The first werewolf picture was about a wolf-girl. It was called *The Werewolf*, and it was made in the United States in 1913. Watuma, a Navajo Indian girl, has been dead for a hundred years. She comes back to life to look for the ghost of the man who had killed her boyfriend. She can't find him until she turns herself into a wolf.

It took a long time to get around to the next

A scene from the first werewolf picture with sound—*The Werewolf of London.* Here is Henry Hull going after a meal. *(Universal, 1935)*

But he did spend quite a lot of time in his laboratory looking for a cure. *(Universal, 1935)*

Right: Lon Chaney, Jr. as *The Wolf Man.* It is said that it took five hours to apply the makeup. *(Universal, 1941)*

Below: Lon Chaney, Jr. as the Wolf Man saved Lou Costello's life in *Abbott and Costello Meet Frankenstein. (Universal, 1948)*

werewolf picture. It was made in 1935, and was called *The Werewolf of London*.

The first really important werewolf film was made in 1941. It was called *The Wolf Man*, and starred Lon Chaney, Jr.

Then the dam burst. Werewolf films have been made in many countries ever since. How many of these have you seen? Most of them are run on television pretty regularly:

Abbott and Costello Meet Frankenstein (American, 1948)
Cry of the Werewolf (American, 1944)
The Curse of the Werewolf (British, 1961)
Dr. Terror's House of Horrors (British, 1964)
The Face of the Screaming Werewolf (Mexican, 1959)
Frankenstein Meets the Wolf Man (American, 1943)
The House of Dracula (American, 1945)
The House of Frankenstein (American, 1944)
I Was a Teenage Werewolf (American, 1957)
The Mad Monster (American, 1941)
She-Wolf of London (American, 1946)
The Undying Monster (American, 1942)
The Werewolf (American, 1956)
Werewolf in a Girl's Dormitory (German, 1961)

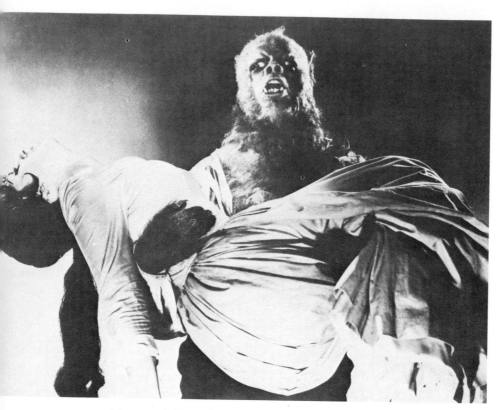

Above: A British version of the Wolf Man picture. Oliver Reed in *The Curse of the Werewolf. (Hammer, 1961)*

Top Right: Bela Lugosi, as the Frankenstein Monster, is irritated with Lon Chaney, Jr., as the Wolf Man, in *Frankenstein Meets the Wolf Man. (Universal, 1943)*

Below Right: In *I Was a Teenage Werewolf,* the sad-faced person under all that hair was Michael Landon. *(American International, 1957)*

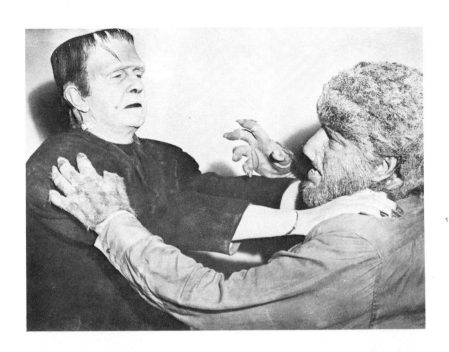

2
WHAT DID IT LOOK LIKE?

Anyone who is superstitious enough to believe in werewolves ought to have an idea of what they look like. Usually, it was believed that a werewolf looked just like any other wolf. It might have been bigger, fiercer, and hungrier than your usual wolf, of course. But there are other differences.

First of all, there were the eyes. Many people thought that they looked just like the eyes of a man or woman—not the slanted eyes of a wolf. And most believers said that its eyes were dry. Maybe this meant that it could not cry.

Others said that the werewolf was paler than a regular wolf. Some said that it had bad eyesight. Still others said that it had no tail.

There were those who thought that its mouth was dry, because it had no saliva there. This probably meant that the werewolf was always thirsty.

One of the strangest beliefs was that the werewolf was clumsier than a real wolf. It fell down a lot. That doesn't sound too fierce, does it?

In some countries, there were easier ways of spotting werewolves. Stories tell of wolves with human hands. Others relate legends of humans with wolf heads. Those would certainly be easy to identify.

Anyway, it was usually hard for the believer to recognize the werewolf in wolf form. But it was not supposed to be as hard to detect it when it was in human form. (Think about your friends and neighbors.) Here is what it was supposed to look like:

Marco Polo was supposed to have come across wolf men
on his travels. Here is an old illustration from a book about
his life. It shows men with wolf heads on the Andaman
Islands, which are located off the coast of India in the Bay
of Bengal.

Look for straight, slanting eyebrows that meet over the bridge of the nose. Notice the curved, reddish fingernails, the extra-long third finger on each hand, and the horrible hairiness, especially on the hands and feet.

To all this, the French believers added hairs on the palms of the hands. They also cautioned against broad hands with short fingers. So, whether you have short or long fingers, you can't win.

In Hungary and parts of the Balkan nations of Yugoslavia, Rumania, Bulgaria, Albania, Greece, and Turkey, werewolves were said to be created by witches. These witches sucked the blood of men born in the time of a new moon.

These poor men had pale, sunken faces, hollow eyes, swollen lips, and flabby, weak arms. This description does not sound as though they were supermen.

But whatever werewolves were supposed to look like, there was a common story about them. Most people thought that they *wanted* to become werewolves.

3

HOW DID IT BECOME
A WEREWOLF?

When the idea of lycanthropy started, people thought that the transformation was caused by witches. They believed that a witch, with the help of the devil, could change into a wolf. Also, he or she could change anyone else into a wolf. There were those who thought that a werewolf was the devil himself, or at least one of his demons.

Tales were told of witches riding wolves to the devil's meetings, and of groups of people changing into wolves. These groups roamed the countryside and attacked farmers.

Sometimes witches were said to change themselves into animals. Here are three witches flying off to a meeting, as shown in a woodcut from 1490.

During the 1500's and 1600's, some people thought that werewolves were in fact witches. They believed that anyone could become a werewolf, just like anyone could become a witch. All you had to do was make a pact with the devil.

But most people believed that a werewolf was just a werewolf. These creatures could not cast spells. They could not utter curses. They could not fly on a broomstick. All they could do was turn into werewolves.

So let's go along with the idea that a werewolf is not a witch. How does he or she turn into a werewolf? People who lived a few hundred years ago had a lot of different ideas.

Some Italians believed that anyone conceived during a new moon would become a werewolf. But there was a shortcut: just sleep on the ground in an open field. This must be done on a Friday night when the moon is full.

But there were lots of other ways:

1. Eat the flesh of a sheep that has been killed by a wolf.
2. Drink water from a wolf's footprint.
3. Drink water from a stream where wolves usually drink.
4. Drink water from certain magical bodies of water. (But these were never put on a map.)
5. Eat a wolf's brain. (Don't knock it until you've tried it.)

Paracelsus, a physician–alchemist–magician of the 1500's, said that anyone who lived an evil life would come back as a wolf after he or she died. But that doesn't make sense, since the werewolf is a living thing and not a ghost.

Paracelsus, a great scientist who believed in werewolves, from a German woodcut of 1567.

In France, there were stories about priests who changed people into werewolves by putting a curse on them. Their victims became wolves for a period of seven years. Other stories tell of the curse of lycanthropy being inherited from parents.

But most people thought that a werewolf really wanted to become a werewolf. He or she brought it on purposefully. Now how did they do it?

Here is a method said to be foolproof. When the moon is full, go to the top of a hill. The moon must then be shining on you. At midnight, draw two magic circles on the ground. The inner circle should be three feet in diameter. The outer circle, which surrounds the inner circle, should have a diameter of seven feet.

In the middle of the inner circle, build a fire. Then place a cauldron over the fire.

The next step is to boil up a brew in the cauldron. Most of the recipes mention henbane, opium, hemlock, or parsley. Others add aconite,

The cauldron over the fire is often used in supernatural procedures. This is from a German woodcut of 1508.

poplar leaves, soot, and fat. Still others contain cowbane, sweet flag, cinquefoil, bat's blood, and deadly nightshade (belladonna). One authority suggested adding flour. That was to thicken the mess.

Then there was a poem to recite. The next step is to smear yourself with the magic ointment from the cauldron. Then drape a wolf's skin over your body. (Hint: some people say that all you need is a wolfskin belt, three fingers wide.)

Next you must wait, and recite another incantation.

Then make a pledge to the Spirit of the Great Unknown.

Now bounce your head on the ground three times and you will become a werewolf. Or so people believed.

If this doesn't work, take out some of the stuff from the cauldron and sprinkle it all over the circles. Then kiss the ground three times. Pick up the cauldron, whirl it around your head, and say another special poem.

What happens next? According to the stories, a long, deep silence will surround you. Then some crashing and banging, groaning and shrieking. And you will feel cold. And be terrified. But who wouldn't be?

Then something is supposed to come to you that will change you into a werewolf. It might be the ghost of a hunter. It might be a monster, half man, half beast. It might be just a shadow or a bit of mist.

But all that is a lot of trouble and there were all kinds of shortcuts available. Some people thought that all you had to do was to roll around in the dust for a while in the light of a full moon. Still others said that you could put on a wolf skin and the change would happen.

Some Irishmen thought that lycanthropy ran in families—that it was passed on from father or mother to son or daughter. And if you were a werewolf you could trace your family tree back to the people who laughed at St. Patrick.

A long time ago, certain Frenchmen said that if you got into trouble with the Church you would turn into a werewolf. This was supposed to be especially true if the priest said nasty things about you from the pulpit.

In the Normandy part of France, you could become a beast if you were kicked out of the Church. The sentence of lycanthropy lasted either three or seven years.

In Lower Brittany, another section of France, all you had to do was to stop taking communion or using holy water. You would turn into a werewolf in ten years.

In Italy, there are several beliefs about becoming a werewolf. It depends on the section of the country you live in.

In Campania, you will be a werewolf during the eight days before Christmas if you were born on Christmas day. In parts of Sicily, be careful that a wolf does not glare at you, or you will become a werewolf.

The Scandinavian countries had more than their fair share of wolves, so they also have a lot of werewolf beliefs.

Norway and Iceland have had many legends of what they called *eigi einhamir*. These were people "not of one skin." In other words, they had the ability to turn themselves into wolves. And sometimes all they had to do was throw a wolf's skin over their bodies.

In Norway and Sweden, the female werewolf was as common as the male. In fact, there was a special routine that was used by women who wanted to change their form.

First, kneel beside a magic river at midnight when the moon is full. Then comes a recitation.

The next step was to bang the forehead three times on the riverbank. Then, dunk the head three times in the water. Be sure to drink a mouthful of water each time. Then wait. And wait. And wait. The whole process took twenty-four hours.

In Poland, there was a legend that hooked up witches, werewolves, *and* weddings.

If the wedding ceremony took place in a house, the witch could sneak up to the front door. Then she would put a girdle of human skin on the threshold. After the wedding, if anyone stepped over the girdle, he or she would become a werewolf.

The story has a happy ending, though. After three years, the witch comes back to the werewolf. She puts a wolf skin over the creature, with the hair side out. Then the werewolf turns back into a human.

But it is said that one time a mistake was made. A witch didn't have a wolf skin big enough to cover the groom. It didn't quite cover his tail. He changed back into a man, all right—but he kept the tail.

In Hungary and the Balkan nations, flowers

were involved in lycanthropy. Supposedly, if you wore a certain flower, you would turn into a werewolf. No one seemed to be able to name this flower. However, it was described as having a bright color (red, yellow, or white), a sticky sap, and a horrible odor. Also it was to be found in damp marshy places.

Some Russians believe in a rather strange method of lycanthropy. First you have to walk through a forest until you find a cut-down tree. Next, stab it with a small copper knife.

Now you must walk around the tree, and repeat a magic verse.

The final step is to jump three times over the tree. And presto! You are a werewolf.

4

WHAT DID IT DO?

There are a lot of stories that connect the werewolf with the celebration of Christmas. In Poland, it was thought that werewolves would go on rampages at that time, and also on Midsummer's Eve, about June 21 or 22.

In the Abruzzi part of Italy, the werewolf is also a Christmas beast. In some parts of Russia, it was thought that werewolves appeared both at Christmas and at the Feast of St. John the Baptist, June 24.

Probably the strangest Christmas werewolf

stories came from a section of Europe that contains the old German state of Prussia, plus Lithuania, Latvia, and Estonia. Here is what was supposed to have happened every Christmas.

All the werewolves would gather together at night. Then they would spread out. First they would raid houses in the woods, trying to break down the doors. If they were successful, they would eat the people inside the houses. Plus all their cattle, sheep, dogs, cats, and every other animal around.

Then they would raid the towns. Their favorite sport seemed to be crashing into taverns. The monsters would empty all the beer and wine kegs on the ground. And then they would pile the barrels one on top of the other in the cellar.

After all of this was over, the werewolves would proceed to a certain ruined castle. Thousands of them would gather and start their games. The trick was for the werewolves to jump over the castle wall. The fattest ones, of

The gathering of were-
wolves. The painting was
the work of Maurice Sand
in 1858.

course, could not make the jump. So they were killed by the others.

Usually, werewolves were thought to be bloodthirsty. In wolf form, they seemed to carry on the typical wolf sports of hunting, killing, and eating. In some places it was believed that they only ate cattle and poultry. But most old stories told of werewolves who were man-eaters.

Supposedly, these creatures ate human flesh. They preferred the meat of children, especially young girls.

A French tale tells of the Wild Beast of Gévaudan. This werewolf was supposed to have roamed over several districts in France between 1764 and 1765.

A group of mounted musketeers were sent out to capture the beast. These men were eager to hunt him, because he had a price of one thousand crowns on his head.

This werewolf was fierce. It was said that he had killed and eaten more than one hundred

Top: One version of what the Wild Beast of *Gé*vaudan looked like. People believed that it could knock humans out with its tail, and it could outrun any other animal. From an engraving of 1765.
Right: Another version of the Wild Beast of Gévaudan. It doesn't look too ferocious in this picture from *The London Magazine* of May, 1765.

people in the region of Languedoc in Southern France alone. There were also stories that he would attack a whole group of armed men without fear.

Thousands tried for months to find him and kill him. Then the King of France demanded his death. At the end, the Wild Beast of Gévaudan was killed by a single archer.

In the Brittany section of France, people used to believe in what was called *le Meneur des Loups*—"the leader of the wolves." He was supposed to be a wizard in human form. His job was to provide shelter and protection for his friends, the werewolves. He was also said to take them out on hikes.

Norway and Sweden had a similar legend. But their belief was that the leader of the wolves was always an old woman.

But not all werewolves were so awful. There actually were some gentle ones, too.

Some of the French werewolves, for example, were not as savage as the Wild Beast of Gévau-

Le Meneur des Loups—a painting by Maurice Sand, 1858.

dan, according to the old stories. There were tales of priests who had been protected by werewolves from wild animals. Other stories told of swimmers who were saved from drowning by werewolves. Even starving travelers were said to have been given food by werewolves.

Jean-Claude vivait en paix : mais il avait des poules et croyait
aux sorciers.

Il va donc un beau jour trouver le père Grenouille, qui passait
pour un de ces derniers, et lui conte :

Qu'il a vu de ses propres yeux, un animal étrange emportant
deux de ses poules.

C'est un *loup-garou*, lui répond le père Grenouille : moyennant
un écu je vous en débarrasserai.

Jean-Claude, rentré chez lui, dort sur ses deux oreilles.

Dès son lever, il va visiter son poulailler : il lui manque
encore deux poules !

Il confie son aventure à un de ses voisins.

Qui lui conseille de mettre un piège à loup devant son
poulailler : ce qu'ils font aussitôt.

Puis ils entrent tous deux chez Jean-Claude.

Et se mettent à jouer aux cartes pour passer le temps.

Ils entendent bientôt des cris vers le poulailler.

Et trouvent dans le piège à loup, le père Grenouille en
Loup-Garou.

LEFT:

A jolly cartoon strip of 1860 by Epinal. The title is *Le Loup-Garou,* or *The Werewolf.* Here is a rough translation of the captions.

FIRST STRIP
Left: Jean-Claude lived in the country: but he had chickens and believed in sorcerers.
Center: One nice day he went to find Father Grenouille, and he told him . . .
Right: . . . that he saw with his own eyes a strange animal taking two of his chickens.

SECOND STRIP
Left: "It is a werewolf," answered Father Grenouille, "For a coin I will get rid of it."
Center: Jean-Claude went home, and slept contentedly.
Right: When he got up he went to visit his chicken coop: he was missing two more chickens!

THIRD STRIP
Left: He told his adventure to one of his neighbors.
Center: He advised him to put a wolf trap in front of his chicken coop: and that he would do the same.
Right: Then the two went into Jean-Claude's house . . .

FOURTH STRIP
Left: . . . and played cards to pass the time.
Center: Then they heard cries from the chicken coop.
Right: In the wolf trap they found Father Grenouille in a werewolf suit.

43

In Spain, there were relatively few legends about werewolves. Apparently the idea of lycanthropy never did catch on too well in that country. The werewolves that were thought to exist seemed to inhabit mountain regions of the country. And they were most often male beasts.

These creatures were said to have inherited their abilities from their fathers. But they must have been gentle fathers, for Spanish werewolves seemed to be more attracted to precious stones than they were to human flesh.

In Portugal, Spain's next-door neighbor, the werewolves were even more gentle. Most of them lived in the southern part of the country, and they did not try to harm anybody. In fact, they were so shy that they were afraid of light. So all anyone needed for protection on a dark road at night was a small candle.

Some Scandinavian werewolves were not the least interested in human flesh, or in any other kind of meat, either. What they really wanted was beer.

Finally, there were gentle werewolf stories that came from White Russia. These creatures did no mischief at all. They were said to rush up to human beings just so that they could lick their hands.

There are all kinds of stories about how to avoid werewolves, cure werewolves, and kill werewolves. Let's look at a few.

5

HOW DO YOU GET RID OF IT?

Very few people who would believe in a werewolf would not want to get rid of the creature. One way or another, it would be a good idea to protect yourself from a werewolf, to kill the werewolf, or, better yet, to cure the werewolf.

As far as self-protection is concerned, there were supposed to be several methods, depending on where you live. For instance, in the Abruzzi region of Italy, a cross can be used. It must be made out of wax, and it must be blessed by a priest. Then a werewolf can't attack you.

In Francoforte, Sicily, you have to be patient.

If a werewolf knocks at the door, just wait. If it knocks for a third time, it is safe to let it in. It will have no power over you. In Messina, Sicily, the protection is simple. Just hit the werewolf with your house key.

Some people thought that werewolves could not come close to running water. So they would build their houses next to a stream.

In the British Isles, it was thought that plants could scare werewolves away. Rye and mistletoe were popular. And you could plant yew and ash trees around your house. They would protect the place from wolf men.

Finally, according to another story, no meat-eating animals would take shelter under the ash tree. That meant protection from both natural meat-eaters and unnatural monsters.

The ash tree was the one with the most magical powers. In ancient Britain, the Christmas log was an ash log. When it was burned, it was supposed to bring good luck to the family of the house.

However, if you couldn't protect yourself from a werewolf, there were many ways of killing the beast. In England and Scotland, they believed in the old silver bullet trick. Shoot it with a silver bullet that has been blessed by a priest and it will not trouble you anymore.

The natives of Normandy, in France, used to think that there was a connection between werewolves and vampires. Suppose that they

The capture of the werewolf of Eschenbach, Germany, from an engraving of 1685. The rooster on the left was put there as bait. The werewolf tried to leap at it, fell in the well, and was hanged by the townsfolk.

found a disturbed grave. They thought that a werewolf was buried in it. So they would dig up the body, chop off its head with an axe that had never been used before, and throw the head into a river or sink it in the sea.

One nice thing about being a werewolf—in most places it is believed that you could be cured. According to some people, all you had to do was go through that complicated ceremony again. But you must do it backwards. Other people believed that you would automatically return to your human shape the next morning after being a werewolf for the night.

Some methods of making a werewolf human again involved bleeding. There was a legend that all one had to do was hit the werewolf three times on the head with a knife. But three drops of blood must be drawn from it at the same time.

In parts of Sicily, the werewolf can also be treated by drawing its blood. But this blood is always black and thick. It is called *sangue pazzo*.

And it always comes out in large, clotted lumps.

In parts of France, the treatment was similar. Just make the werewolf bleed. It doesn't matter how, or from where. Bleeding alone will cure the creature.

Talking was sometimes used as a cure. In the German section of Schleswig-Holstein, it was said that if the werewolf were called by its baptismal name, it would be cured. And in parts of Denmark, all you had to do was shout and accuse it of being a werewolf.

There were those who believed that if a werewolf lost part of its body in a fight, that part would turn back into its human form. Here is an old French tale that serves as a good example.

One day, while he was in the woods, a hunter was attacked by a wolf. He managed to cut off one of the paws of the animal, and the wolf ran away.

He put the paw in his pack as a souvenir of the battle. But on the way home, the hunter ran into a friend. Wanting to brag, he pulled out the paw to show it off. Imagine his surprise when he saw the hand of a woman. And there was a fine gold ring on one of the fingers.

But he was even more startled when he finally got home. He found that his own wife had mysteriously lost her own left hand. There she stood, dripping blood. Later, she was executed for lycanthropy.

One of the strangest ways to cure a werewolf was very complicated, too. First open a vein in the beast and let the blood drain until it has fainted. Then feed it wholesome food and bathe it in fresh water. Sprinkle it with whey for three days, and feed it laxatives.

After three days, the dosing begins. Use the following: dodder of thyme, epithymus, aloes, wormwood, squills, poley, slender birthwort, phlebotomy, and cataplasms. (Who knows what most of those things are?)

Then make the beast drink vinegar. If all this doesn't work, make it vomit by forcing it to drink hellebore and by rubbing its nostrils with opium. Maybe the cure is worse than the disease.

Other cures for lycanthropy required a little patience. The Roman historian, Pliny, suggested that the werewolf should jump into water. Then, when it comes out, it should eat no meat for nine years. That would guarantee a cure.

Another suggestion was to have the werewolf kneel in the same spot for one hundred years. After all that time, it would never again return to its wolf form. That one was a story told in Lithuania.

In parts of Greece, it was believed that you had to be extra cautious if you were not cured of being a werewolf. If you died in wolf form, you would become a vampire.

In Serbia, just find the wolf skin hanging on a tree while the werewolf is in human form. Burn the skin, and the creature will be cured.

There have been a lot of people who were accused of being werewolves. What did they do, and what happened to them?

6

WERE THERE REAL
WEREWOLVES?

In the 1500's and 1600's there were quite a few cases of lycanthropy reported. And many of them were brought to trial. Let's take a look at a few of the more famous, and find out what happened to them.

The first trial to be considered took place in France. In December of 1521, two men were arrested in the town of Poligny. Pierre Burgot and Michel Verdun were said to be werewolves. The beginning of the story went back a number of years.

In the year 1502, there was a fair in the town of Poligny. And on that day, Burgot, a shepherd, was trying very hard to round up his sheep. He wanted to go to the fair, and, besides, there was a fierce storm coming up.

There he was, running around the field, when three men on horseback rode up to him. The horses were black and the men were dressed all in black. Burgot said he was trying to get his sheep together and one of the riders offered to help.

The horseman said that if Burgot would be loyal to him, his sheep would be saved. The shepherd agreed and all the sheep were captured.

Then the strange part of the story was told by Burgot. He was forced to kneel down and swear to be loyal to the man in black. He swore that he would never worship God again. Also, he promised never to go to mass or use holy water. And he renounced his own baptism.

The years went by, and Burgot began to forget

what he had promised. Then he met Michel Verdun, who claimed to be a witch. Verdun took Burgot to a witches' meeting and put some ointment on the two of them. They immediately turned into werewolves, it was said.

The two of them went on a rampage. They killed and tore to pieces a twelve-year-old boy. The next victim was a woman who was picking peas in her garden. Eventually, they were said to have killed several people, most of them young girls.

Then Verdun made a mistake. He picked on a man who was able to wound him. Verdun ran back to his house and had his wife bandage him up. But the man he had attacked had followed him through the woods. Verdun, in human form, was captured and told the police about Burgot.

Verdun and Burgot also told about another werewolf, a man named Philibert Montot. All three confessed to the crime of lycanthropy. All three were convicted and executed.

France was the location of another werewolf trial in 1573. This trial was held in the village of Dôle. The culprit was named Gilles Garnier, and he was said to have eaten several children while he was in the form of a wolf. One horrible part of the story is that he was accused of taking some of the leftovers home to his wife.

After several more murders, he started to commit his crimes in human form. He was discovered as he was about to eat a young boy. Garnier had dragged the child into the woods and strangled him. Some strangers who were walking by chased him away from the body.

Garnier was eventually captured by the people of the village. At his trial, "The Hermit of Dôle" confessed to everything. One odd thing about Garnier's attitude, however. These events took place at a time when Roman Catholics could not eat meat on Friday. And Garnier seemed to be sorrier about eating the boy on a Friday than about having committed the murder. Garnier was burned alive for his crimes.

A sixteenth-century German engraving showing a werewolf attacking a man.

Another famous werewolf trial was held in
Germany in 1589. The culprit was a man named
Peter Stubb (also known as Stump, Stumpf,
Stube, Stubbe, or Stub). Spelling was a little
casual in those days, so let's stick with Stubb for
our story.

It was said that the devil himself made Stubb
a werewolf. He was given a wolfskin belt and
immediately began acting like a werewolf. According to a book published in 1590, he prac-

ticed "his malice on men, women, and children, in the shape of some beast, whereby he might live without dread of danger of life, and unknown to be the executor of any bloody enterprise, which he meant to commit."

For twenty-five years he terrified everyone. Sometimes he killed livestock or men he didn't like. But most of the time he preyed on women and children. It was said that he even killed his own son.

The people of the village of Bedburg chased him, of course. But he wasn't caught for all those twenty-five years. At last he was caught by a group of men and their hunting dogs.

The story goes that Stubb tried to throw off his wolfskin belt so he would turn back into a man. And the men chasing him said that they saw him regain his human shape. Then they grabbed him and took him to trial on a charge of lycanthropy.

Stubb confessed to everything. And his execution was horrible. It was slow and it was

Above: Illustrations from *The Damnable Life of One Stubbe Peeter*, 1590. Peter Stubb was supposed to be a werewolf. The townspeople tried to catch him . . . and eventually were successful.

Above: Stubb was tortured . . . and beheaded . . .

Right: . . . and then burned at the stake with his daughter and his girlfriend.

painful. After he was dead, his head was mounted on a pole outside the town, and the rest of his body was burned.

On that very same day, Peter Stubb's daughter and his girlfriend were also burned at the stake. They had been accused of helping Stubb with his crimes.

Back to France for the story of the man-wolf of Caude. His name was Jacques Rollet, and he was tried in 1598. The body of a fifteen-year-old boy had been found near a forest. It was horribly mangled, and the villagers who discovered it said that they had seen three wolves run into the forest as they neared the corpse.

The people decided to chase the wolves, but they found someone else—a half-naked man roaming through the woods. He had long hair and a beard. His hands were covered with blood. Later, pieces of human flesh were found under his fingernails. It was Jacques Rollet.

Rollet confessed to that murder and to the murders of several others. It was a strange list.

He claimed to have killed women and court bailiffs. He also said that he didn't care much for the bailiffs, because their flesh was tough and tasteless.

But Rollet was lucky. He was not executed for his crimes. The court quite rightly decided that he was crazy, and sentenced him to a madhouse for two years.

In 1603, in the Gascony section of France, children began disappearing mysteriously. A baby had even been taken from its cradle.

A thirteen-year-old girl, Marguerite Poirier, told a strange tale. She had been attacked, she said, by a wolf. It had happened in the middle of the day, but there was a full moon in the sky. Marguerite was taking care of some cattle at the time. And she was able to drive away the wolf with her staff.

Jean Grenier, a boy of about thirteen, bragged that he was a werewolf. And that he was the one who had bothered Marguerite. He also claimed to have eaten three or four other children and a few dogs. Jean seemed really to believe that he could change into a wolf.

Jeanne Gaboriaut, an eighteen-year-old girl, also accused Grenier. Jeanne was also watching some cattle when Grenier came up to her and said that he wanted to marry her. She told him, she said, that he was "sallow and dirty." Then he said, "Ah, that is because of the wolf's skin I wear."

Grenier also made another strange confession. He said that he had met a "gentleman of the forest," Pierre Labourat. Labourat, riding a black horse, had brought Jean a wolf skin and a special salve to rub all over his body. This changed him into a wolf.

Grenier claimed to travel in a wolf pack with eight other werewolves. This happened three times a week, on Mondays, Fridays, and Saturdays. He and his friends hunted at twilight and just before dawn.

Jean Grenier was arrested and tried for his crimes. But the judge took into account his unhappy life. Jean had been deserted by his parents when he was very young, so he had to turn to begging to support himself. There was also a suspicion that he was crazy. So he was confined to a Franciscan friary, where he lived a good life until he died seven years later.

In 1847 and 1848, there was another werewolf episode in France. Cemeteries in Paris were vandalized and bodies were torn from their graves. Some of these bodies looked as if they had been chewed on. At one of these cemeteries, the Père-Lachaise, a creature had reportedly been seen. It was described as being half-man, half-animal. The witnesses said that it vanished into thin air, and that dogs howled and refused to go near the spot where it had last been seen.

A trap was set, and the creature was caught. He was Francois Bertrand, a sergeant in the French Army. He was only twenty-five years old.

Bertrand confessed to the grave robberies, and told of his early life. When he was a lonely young boy, he really loved animals; gradually he changed, however, and he began to search for the bodies of dead animals.

After he joined the army, Bertrand began digging up graves and mauling the bodies that he found. But he never attacked a living person, he said. "I was very gentle to everybody. I couldn't have harmed a child."

The court decided that Bertrand was suffering from a mental disease in which he thought he was an animal. But he was not a murderer, so his sentence was only for one year.

These have been some stories about people who thought that they were werewolves. But how about those men and women who turned into other kinds of animals?

7
WERE THERE OTHERS?

There are many places in the world where you won't hear any werewolf tales. That's probably because there aren't wolves there. But there are other choices. What about were-lions, were-tigers, were-bears, were-foxes, were-hyenas, were-boars, were-jaguars, and many more?

In India, for example, legends of were-serpents and were-apes are popular. And there are a lot of stories about were-tigers. One of them is about a man who could turn into a tiger anytime he wanted to. But he needed someone to repeat a certain spell while he was in tiger

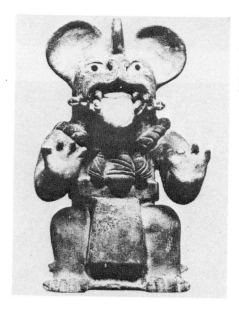

A pottery figure of the
Mexican god Tezcatlipoca.
He is shown as a were-
jaguar.

form. Otherwise he couldn't return to his
human shape.

He taught the spell to a friend. Things worked
out well for a time, but then the friend died. So
the man taught the spell to his wife.

One day he was in tiger form. After he had
eaten a couple of antelopes, he decided to
change back into a man. So he trotted up to his
wife, hoping that she would repeat the spell.

But she didn't recognize him, and she began

to scream. The tiger jumped around, trying to remind his wife that she had to help him. But this only made her more nervous and she still didn't recognize her husband.

Finally the were-tiger lost his temper. He killed the woman.

It took a while, but he realized how stupid he had been. He had no one left who could help him turn back into a man. According to the story, he was so angry with himself that he turned into a real killer. From then on, he killed men wherever and whenever he could.

Legends of were-tigers are common in Cambodia as well. Both men and women are said to be able to change magically into these creatures. But while a man can change immediately, it takes a little longer for the woman to transform herself.

The woman must be smeared with magic salves. After that, she runs into the woods. But she is still in human form. It takes her seven days to change into a tiger.

There is a way of stopping the change during these seven days. A man of the village is rubbed with the same salve. Then he goes into the forest to find the woman. If he finds her, there is an easy way of breaking the spell: he hits her over the head with a heavy club.

Ethiopia, in particular, is full of were-hyena stories. It is said that one day a servant asked his master if he could take the day off. The master agreed, and immediately the servant turned himself into a hyena and ran off into the jungle.

In some parts of Africa, the belief in were-lions was especially strong. According to some legends, the were-lion's transformation takes place when a lion's body is taken over by the spirit of a dead tribal chief.

It is often said that there is an easy way to tell a real lion from a were-lion: the were-lion can't stand the smell of gunpowder. But how you get close enough to test this idea is not explained.

In some parts of the Orient, there are legends

The Japanese had stories about were-cats, too. This is a
painting by the famous artist, Kuniyoshi.

of were-foxes. Some Chinese used to believe that a normal fox could live to be about eight hundred years old. But by the time that the fox got to be about five hundred years old, he could turn into a human being if he wanted to. So not all were-animal stories are about humans who turn into animals; this one is about an animal who turns into a human.

In some parts of the Orient, a fox has to go to a lot of trouble if it wants to turn into a human. First, it must find a skull on a grassy plain. Then it has to wear the skull on its head. Then it has to face north and begin to pray to the North Star.

At first there are quiet prayers. But after a while, the prayers are shouted and the fox must make violent jumping motions. And, if the trick is to be successful, the skull must stay on the head during the whole ceremony.

But that is not all. The whole thing must be repeated one hundred times. And each time, the skull must not fall off the fox's head or it has to begin all over again. Then if the fox is successful for the hundreth time, it will turn into a man.

But what if the fox wants to turn into a woman? The poor thing must go through all the things that have been mentioned, as well as other requirements: it must live for the rest of its life near a graveyard.

There were stories of how to change back into a real fox, if you should become a were-fox. Smell the smoke from a burning refuse pile. Or drink weak tea. Or swallow roasted leaves.

And the were-fox can change back if it can get some people to help. They must fumigate and then bathe the animal. Or they can sic their dogs on the poor creature.

By the way, do you want to protect yourself from were-foxes? Just carry a tortoise foot in your left hand at all times.

People in other parts of the world believed in the were-bear. There was a story from Spain of the 1600's. It seemed that a Spanish nobleman ate a bear's brain. He immediately turned into a bear and went off to the hills to search for food.

Some Spaniards thought that there was a poison in a bear's brain. So if you boiled the brain and distilled it into a liquid, you could drink it. Then you would turn into a bear.

Russia seemed to be a hotbed of were-animals. In addition to the were-bear, some peasants believed in the were-eagle, the were-elk, and the were-boar.

The were-boar was a favorite in Bulgaria, too. Some people there believed that Turks who had never eaten pork would become were-boars when they die.

So, people from all over the world have had their legends about were-animals. Some Scandinavians still believe in the were-bear. And some people in Greece even now believe in the were-boar and the were-dog.

In East Africa there is a belief in the were-hyena. In the rest of Africa there are tales of were-leopards, were-jaguars, were-lions, were-elephants, were-crocodiles, and even were-

Above: How about a were-reindeer from Lapland?

Below: The "su," a sort of were-opposum, from the southern tip of South America.

sharks. Java, Borneo, Malaysia, China, Japan, and the West Indies are also full of were-animal stories.

Some Indians of North America believed in a were-bison. In Central and South America, you would hear of the were-tiger, the were-jaguar, the were-eagle, and the were-serpent.

And there are many more—mammals, birds, amphibians, reptiles, and fish. There were even were-worms and examples of other lower forms of life. There must have been some reasons for these strange ideas. Let us examine a few.

8

SOME REAL
EXPLANATIONS

All kinds of scientists have given us reasons why so many people have believed in were-wolves and other were-animals. People who study medicine, psychology, folklore, anthropology, and even pharmacology have offered opinions.

Folklorists and anthropologists tell of strange groups of people in history. There was an ancient Greek cult that worshipped Lycaeon, (see page 5), the man whose legend may have started the whole thing. These Greeks held

A nineteenth-century painting of the berserkers in action.

strange ceremonies in which they wore wolf masks. And they chased animals or even men.

The story goes that when they caught their prey, they would tear it to pieces. Suppose you were living at the time and were quite superstitious. You might believe that these madmen had actually changed themselves into wolves.

Then there were the Scandinavian believers. Everyone knows about the Vikings, of course. But there was an extra-fierce group of Vikings called the berserkers. (The word, berserker, comes from two Norse words, *bear sark*, or bear skin.) These men believed that if they dressed in the skin of a beast that they had killed, they would become braver. They would take on the ferocity of the dead animal. So they often wore wolf skins.

The berserkers were famous for invading peaceful towns in lightning-like raids. They would howl, foam at the mouth, and bite on their shields. They were so fierce during battle that they acted like wild animals.

Now suppose you were observing one of these raids. At the time of the berserkers, you probably would have been very superstitious. You probably could not read and write. And you would be willing to believe in almost anything.

Here comes a group of men wearing animal skins. They act like animals. They scream and yell. They froth at the mouth. And they kill everyone in sight. Wouldn't it be easy to believe that these men were really wolves or bears in human form?

Fortunately, berserkers, like werewolves, could be cured. Legend has it that they could be rid of their evil ways if they were baptized in the Church.

There is a psychological reason for the belief in were-animals, too. Look at how many people confessed so readily that they were werewolves. Could they have been insane? There is a mental disease called lycanthropy. Those who have this disease often think that they are animals. They may even howl. They may crave raw meat.

Some people who thought that they were werewolves did not change from human form. This is a drawing by the sixteenth-century German artist, Lucas Cranach.

They may even run around on all fours during an attack of this sickness.

Fortunately, by the end of the Middle Ages, people began to realize that when a hairy man began growling and saying he was a wolf, he was probably insane. After all, he didn't actually turn into a wolf. Since people, by that time, recognized lycanthropy as a mental disorder, some of the victims were not as cruelly treated as before.

Records of trials in the late Middle Ages show that there were many persons convicted of being werewolves. But the sentences changed. Instead of being burned at the stake, they were often sent to mental institutions or monasteries.

There probably were a few imagined werewolves who were not insane, though. They might have been under the influence of drugs. Remember all the things that were used in the magic salve that was supposed to change you into a werewolf?

Belladonna, also called deadly nightshade, was often used. This is a poisonous plant that can make people wildly excited. It can also cause delirious dreams.

Sometimes poppy seeds were used. Opium comes from poppy seeds.

Hemlock was another favorite ingredient. It is also poisonous. And some people say that the parsley used in some of the recipes is really hemlock.

Finally, remember the old gypsy woman in

Frankenstein Meets the Wolf Man? She kept
repeating a little ditty:

> Many a man who is pure in heart
> and says his prayers by night
> May become a wolf when the wolfsbane blooms
> and the moon is shining bright.

That's the old gypsy woman, Maria Ouspenskaya, telling
Lon Chaney, Jr., that he is a werewolf. Frankenstein's
monster looks on. *(Universal, 1943)*

Aconite, another popular part of the salve, is another name for the wolfsbane in the old woman's poem. Aconite is a poison that slows down the heartbeat.

These plants are all poisonous. And they would have killed anyone who drank the stuff. But the future werewolf didn't drink it—he or she rubbed it on the skin. Suppose that the potion was rubbed in hard enough so that some of it could enter the bloodstream. The person wouldn't die, but an effect would be felt.

So, the combinations in the salve might produce a mentally confused person. There might be a slowed-down heartbeat. The victim might have lazy body movements, or become dizzy and short of breath. He or she might also become excited and delirious.

Remember that this poor soul *wanted* to turn into a werewolf. With all these strange things going on in the body, isn't it possible that such an unfortunate might think that he or she *had* become a werewolf?

Finally, there is a medical explanation for a belief in lycanthropy. Those who were thought to be werewolves may have been suffering from a disease. Two of these diseases are hypertrichosis and porphyria.

Hypertrichosis in medical terms is correctly called *Hypertrichosis universalis congenita*. It is a genetic disease; that means that it is passed on from parent to child. You can't get it if someone sneezes on you. And if you have it, you would know it by now. So don't worry.

Very soon after birth, a baby with hypertrichosis will grow long hair on its ears. Later, silky hair appears which can be four to ten inches in length. This hair can be found on all parts of the body except for the palms of the hand, the soles of the feet, the ends of the fingers and toes, and the lips. It's a good thing that this disease occurs only about one time in each billion births.

People with hypertrichosis are often missing their back teeth. This means that they must chew with the front teeth, which gives them a dog-like appearance.

Combine the hairiness with the table manners of a dog, and you can almost believe that these poor creatures are werewolves.

These people are not mental defectives, however. One person who had the disease was named Peter Gonzales. He was born in 1556, and soon after, long dark hair began to grow all over his body. The hair on his face was especially long. He couldn't see unless it was curled out of the way.

A hairy woman, probably suffering from hypertrichosis. (Pen and ink sketch by Virginia Aylesworth)

What do you do with a person like that? At the time, many kings in Europe collected freaks to be used to entertain the members of the court. So Peter was sent to the court of Henry II of France.

Gonzales soon became a favorite of King Henry because he was so witty and intelligent. The king even hired a tutor for him to improve his education. Peter was also permitted to marry a very pretty girl. Gonzales and his wife went on a grand tour of Europe. Peter even served as an emissary of the king.

It is recorded that at least three of Peter Gonzalez's children were hairy. And at least one of the three passed on the hairiness to the next generation.

Now for the disease called porphyria. People who have this disease are sensitive to light. Many of them cannot bear to go out into the daylight because it hurts their eyes so badly.

They also have **sores** on their skin. And these sores may break open.

They develop into very hairy people. And the color of their skin may change, most often to a yellow color.

Then, too, their teeth may turn reddish in color. Another common symptom is mental disorder. Finally, they may go into convulsions from time to time.

What a sad picture. Here is a person who is most often seen at night because he or she cannot stand the sun. This person has yellowish skin, running sores, reddish teeth, a lot of hair, and may go into convulsions right in front of your eyes. If you met the poor creature some night in a dark alley, might you not think that you had run across a werewolf?

So there are some explanations of why people believed in werewolves and other were-animals. These creatures never did exist, of course. But there was a time when most men and women in the world were prepared to believe almost anything. And some still do.

OTHER BOOKS
ABOUT WEREWOLVES

IN FOLKLORE

Aylesworth, Thomas G. *Werewolves and Other Monsters*. Reading, Massachusetts: Addison-Wesley Publishing Company, Incorporated, 1971.

Bayless, Raymond. *Animal Ghosts*. New York: University Books, Incorporated, 1970.

Baring-Gould, Sabine. *The Book of Werewolves*. New York: Causeway Books, 1973.

Cohen, Daniel. *Ghostly Animals*. Garden City, New York: Doubleday & Company, Incorporated, 1977.

———. *A Natural History of Unnatural Things*. New York: The McCall Publishing Company, 1971.

Farson, Daniel. *Vampires, Zombies, and Monster Men*. Garden City, New York: Doubleday & Company, Incorporated, 1976.

Garden, Nancy. *Werewolves*. Philadelphia: J.B. Lippincott Company, 1973.

Godwin, John. *Unsolved: The World of the Unknown*. Garden City, New York: Doubleday & Company, Incorporated, 1976.

Hamel, Frank. *Human Animals*. New Hyde Park, New York: University Books, 1969.

Hill, Douglas, and Pat Williams. *The Supernatural*. New York: Hawthorn Books, Incorporated, 1965.

McHargue, Georgess. *Meet the Werewolf*. Philadelphia: J.B. Lippincott Company, 1975.

O'Donnell, Elliott. *Werewolves*. New York: Longvue Press, 1965.

Summers, Montague. *The Werewolf*. New Hyde Park, New York: University Books, 1966.

IN THE MOVIES

Aylesworth, Thomas G. *Monsters from the Movies*. Philadelphia: J.B. Lippincott Company, 1972.
————. *Movie Monsters*. Philadelphia: J.B. Lippincott Company, 1975.

Edelson, Edward. *Great Monsters of the Movies*. Garden City, New York: Doubleday & Company, Incorporated, 1973.

Manchel, Frank. *Terrors of the Screen*. Englewood Cliffs, New Jersey: Prentice-Hall, Incorporated, 1970.

IN LITERATURE

Endore, Guy. *The Werewolf of Paris*. New York: Pocket Books, 1941.

INDEX